# Doin' All Things

PHIL. 4:13

## WHEN LIFE HURTS

# Andrea Mitchell

ELOHAI
INTERNATIONAL
PUBLISHING & MEDIA

Copyright 2021© Andrea Mitchell

All rights reserved. No part of this book may be reproduced or transmitted in any form, without the written permission of the author, except for brief quotations for review purposes.

Published by ELOHAI International Publishing & Media:
P.O. Box 64402
Virginia Beach, VA 23467
elohaipublishing.com

For inquiries or to request bulk copies, e-mail hello@elohaiintl.com.

ELOHAI International publishes stories that demonstrate the redemptive power of God. The information in this book is true and complete to the best of the author's knowledge. Any advice, memories, or recommendations are made without guarantee on the part of the author or publisher. The author and publisher disclaim any liability in connection with the use of this information.

Unless otherwise noted, scripture taken from the New King James Version®. Copyright© 1982 by Thomas Nelson. Used by permission. All rights reserved.

Scriptures marked KJV are taken from the KING JAMES VERSION (KJV): KING JAMES VERSION, public domain.

Scripture quotations marked (NIV) are taken from the Holy Bible, New International Version®, NIV®. Copyright © 1973, 1978, 1984, 2011 by Biblica, Inc.™ Used by permission of Zondervan. All rights reserved worldwide. www.zondervan.com. The "NIV" and "New International Version" are trademarks registered in the United States Patent and Trademark Office by Biblica, Inc.™

Scripture quotations are from the ESV® Bible (The Holy Bible, English Standard Version®), copyright © 2001 by Crossway, a publishing ministry of Good News Publishers. Used by permission. All rights reserved.

ISBN: 978-1-953535-16-0

Printed in the United States of America

# Dedication

*This book is dedicated to anyone currently going through a storm and struggling with keeping the faith while maintaining the courage to move forward with Doin' All Things.*

# Acknowledgments

*I would like to acknowledge my tribe built on family and friends who have been with me through this journey.
To my mother, Rosalind Wilson Davis; thank you for life, for your support and your example of how to be a strong black woman and mother. To my sister, Aerielle Boyd, the wisest big little sister ever, thank you for your prayers and showing me how to see things from a different perspective.*

# Table of Contents

**Prologue** . . . . . . . . . . . . . . . . . . . . . . . . . . . . . . . . . . . . . . . ix

**Chapters**
1. Questioning God . . . . . . . . . . . . . . . . . . . . . . . . . . . . . . 1
2. A Time to Grieve . . . . . . . . . . . . . . . . . . . . . . . . . . . . . 11
3. Rooted in Faith . . . . . . . . . . . . . . . . . . . . . . . . . . . . . . 21
4. Fear Not . . . . . . . . . . . . . . . . . . . . . . . . . . . . . . . . . . . . 31
5. Stop The Thoughts at the Door . . . . . . . . . . . . . . . . . . 45
6. Wait Upon The Lord . . . . . . . . . . . . . . . . . . . . . . . . . . 53
7. Letting Go of Anger and Forgiving Others . . . . . . . . . 63
8. Forgiveness . . . . . . . . . . . . . . . . . . . . . . . . . . . . . . . . . 71
9. Prayer Changed Me . . . . . . . . . . . . . . . . . . . . . . . . . . 79
10. Self-Care . . . . . . . . . . . . . . . . . . . . . . . . . . . . . . . . . . . 89
11. It is Well with My Soul . . . . . . . . . . . . . . . . . . . . . . . . 95
12. Moving Forward . . . . . . . . . . . . . . . . . . . . . . . . . . . . 103

**Scripture Index** . . . . . . . . . . . . . . . . . . . . . . . . . . . . . . . 105
**Resources** . . . . . . . . . . . . . . . . . . . . . . . . . . . . . . . . . . 107
**Stay Connected** . . . . . . . . . . . . . . . . . . . . . . . . . . . . . . 109

# Prologue

In September of 2020, a tragic event was revealed to me and it changed the trajectory of my life and marriage forever. As a result of this event, I felt it was no longer healthy nor safe for me or my girls to be around my husband and he had to leave our home immediately. Three days after receiving this devastating news, the reality of the situation of my future and family's future set in. Anger, sadness, fear, depression and anxiety had kicked in overdrive and of course my emotions were everywhere and rightfully so. The trust had been broken and violated. Only God Himself could repair this. I allowed myself to cry and pray and cry and pray. Then, with a prompting from the Holy Spirit, I began to cry, pray, and write.

As I began to cry and pray, the spiritual purpose began to manifest. I realized that God could and would get the glory from this situation and it would not break me. As a woman of faith, two things became all too clear to me: the Lord answered my prayer regarding a situation that I had been praying about for some time now; and two: this experience was attached to my mission and life's branding "Doin' All Things," which happens to be the name of my new business.

Philippians 4:13 says, "I can do all things through Christ who strengtheneth me." As believers, we do not get to simply quote scripture, or in my case, develop and sell faith-based statement t-shirts, without walking the walk. This situation forced me to truly live out my brand, depend on Christ, and see whether or not I could really do *all things* through Christ as He gives me strength.

When you give your life to Christ, salvation is not just for you alone. You become a vessel and your purpose is to bring others to Christ, and that is pretty much by any means necessary. So as I began to write this, even during my tears, and only two weeks into this hell of a life-changing battle, I knew it was all for Him. I'm still Doin' All Things in His name, through His strength, and for His glory.

Before the turn of events that prompted this book, everything was as fine as it could have been given the fact that we are living through a pandemic (COVID-19) and a worldwide epidemic. I am a wife and mother of two beautiful girls. All marriages have their trials, and all families have their issues, but from my perspective, everything was fine. We had just returned from a family getaway out of town. Nothing could have prepared me for what happened when I returned home. Due to the pandemic, my family was pretty much confined to our house for months on end. It has been a challenging time for everybody. The kids have had to get used to being online, and my husband and I had to get used to being with each other twenty-four-seven, and we also had my mother-in-law come live with us. Aside from that, I still considered us very blessed. We hadn't lost our jobs. All of our bills were paid, and my husband was even able to get a promotion. Despite going through pandemic-related challenges like everyone else during this time, including not being able to do the things we used to do, we were still very blessed. Many people were (and still are) dealing with mental health battles that may have intensified during this pandemic, and so I know that part of the reason why I have been led to write is to provide words of comfort and solutions that lead to strength and healing.

This book will speak to a number of uncomfortable topics in an effort to help people of all ages and walks of life, who might be dealing with many of the issues I've had to confront during this time. I've had to fight through depression, anxiety, fear, grief and loss, and break generational curses all while making life-altering decisions for the sake of my children. This book will also give insight to those seeking to break toxic cycles to aid in their deliverance process from addictive behaviors.

In dealing with my pain, I realized that a lot of people think they know how they would handle a difficult situation, but truth be told, a lot of times you will not know until you are confronted with the situation head on. I chose to place the well being of my children and my peace above everything else. I chose to use this painful season of my life to show the world that even during the storm, God is still good. The root of the problem in this situation was that I was affected by the battles and demons that my husband faced because he did not deal with them properly. His approach consisted of self-medicating in more ways than one. I turned a blind eye to his practices for years and thought my love and prayers would carry him and us through. And it did for a season, but not the lifetime like I had vowed. One of the biggest lessons I learned from this experience was that when you don't have the tools and strength to fight your battles, you turn to other methods that will lead you down dangerous roads that are hard to turn away from. Most of the tools we need to fight are found in a life with Christ and the Word of God.

My prayer is for this book to provide encouraging, practical, and biblical tools to people who are experiencing battles with mental health, grief and loss, trauma, and fear so they don't have to take matters into their own hands. I want to provide the tools needed to break generational curses so that we no longer have to try to numb and ignore pain. In the black community, trauma and tragedy are all too often swept under the rug never to be spoken about. This is exactly how the pattern of self medicating and avoidance begins to include a lineage of generational curses resulting in dysfunctionality within families.

While we are on the subject of generational curses and unstable families, let's be honest and clear here, these behaviors and attitudes are not linked to just one racial or ethnic community. The Bible speaks of dysfunctional families from the very beginning with Adam following Eve's lead and their disobedience bringing forth years of pain for women and the fall of the human race. Then there was Abraham and Sarah who struggled with fertility issues for years and finally decided to take matters into their own hands instead of waiting on God. There was also Jacob and Esau who were put against one another by their own mother for the sake of an inheritance! Generational curses, iniquities, and family dysfunction exist in every family, but we do not have to continue this routine. Our generation has the power to break the cycle.

Prayerfully, *Doin All Things When Life Hurts* will help you identify the God-given resources and tools available to you to confront the issues that are plaguing your life and family so that you can enjoy the abundant life of everlasting peace *"that surpasses all understanding"* that only our Savior Jesus Christ came to provide.

# Helpful Tips to Use this Book

The beginning of each section/chapter begins with my raw thoughts experienced during this hard time. Afterwards, we go into a section where you, as the reader, will be prompted to consider various scriptural truths and life lessons. At the end of each section there is a prompt called, "Do the Hard Part." Take a moment on the journal lines and pages that follow to complete each exercise honestly so that you can work through the difficult aspects of your situation. When you "Do the Hard Part," God will step in and do His part.

# Chapter One
## Questioning God

"For I know the plans I have for you," declares the Lord, "plans to prosper you and not to harm you, plans to give you hope and a future."

---

Jeremiah 29:11 (NIV)

*At the very beginning of the pandemic when the state where I lived was put on lockdown, I anointed all the doorways of our home with oil. After all of the anointing oil that I put around the house and around the family members inside of the house, how the hell could God let this happen? I was reminded by my big little sister (she's seven years younger than me, but so wise) that the oil was not a promise that bad things wouldn't happen, but a show of my faith that regardless of the circumstances, God was still in control. Her words were full of wisdom and truth but they didn't stop the pain nor me questioning God's methods for getting my husband's attention. See back during the summer, I began to pray consistently over my husband and some of his choice ways for dealing with his mental health, and suddenly my prayers had been answered… just not how I was expecting.*

It's always easy to give God credit when things are going well. We are all too eager to yell "Won't' He Do It!" when the blessings are flowing abundantly. However, the minute something negative and unexpected happens, we question Him and His work ethics. It's just inevitable to question God during hard times. I questioned the oil that was put on my home because of the turmoil I was currently enduring. As I was praying for healing one morning, He spoke to me and said, "If I have answered your prayer regarding your husband, what makes you think that I won't answer your prayer for healing for all of you?" He had already answered me, yet I was still questioning in my spirit: how am I going to heal from this? How will my children heal from this? Even though this wasn't my fault, will they forgive me? Will they even forgive my husband for that matter? I've never been known to be a bitter or hateful person and I certainly didn't want my girls to be this way either. It was and still is imperative that they also know for themselves even as young children that God is all knowing and that despite this ugly situation, His presence is still with us.

Questioning God often can contribute to a lack of trust in God based on what we are currently seeing with our natural eyes. Even those who have a solid relationship with God will ultimately question Him. Others may have a hard time trusting God because of past experiences that didn't go the way they wanted or because they simply have yet to have a real encounter with Him—period.

Common questions and statements people say to God during hard times are:

1. I thought you loved me, God?

2. Why are the answers to my prayers taking so long?

3. How could you let this happen?

4. I bet if I was out in the world, this wouldn't have happened.

5. You know I can't handle this God. This is why I have a hard time believing in You because things like this happen.

If you are familiar with the Bible story of Abraham and Sarah, you will recall a moment during Sarah's season of waiting to be a mother, she overheard a conversation between Abraham and the Lord. She listened in and heard the Lord reveal to Abraham that she would still bring forth a child even in her late stage of life. She laughed at the thought of having a child at that age, ultimately questioning God. God being all knowing then in turn questioned her for not believing He could do the impossible! He challenged and assured her that in due season she would deliver a son, and she did. At the age of ninety, Sarah gave birth to Issac, the child she prayed for even after taking matters into her own hands when she created her own surrogacy and instructed her maid to sleep with her husband.

Questioning God during hard times is human nature, however as you mature in your walk with God, you will question less and thank Him more especially during dark moments. We are not alone with our thoughts of questioning the how's and why's of God's work and His methods of choice. However questioning God not only shows our lack of trust, it also puts more of the focus on the problem and belittles our faith in Him. This is the point in our lives when we should be increasing our faith with the word.

Increasing your faith in God is accomplished through prayer and by staying in the word! God is not a genie in a bottle only granting three wishes. He doesn't just answer one prayer. He answers all of your prayers in due time when He sees fit just like He did with Sarah. The waiting period for answered prayers are simply "Count it All Joy" moments to build your patience, and at the same time, it allows you the opportunity to draw closer to Him.

> *"So then faith comes by hearing, and hearing by the word of God."*
>
> Romans 10:17

> *"For we walk by faith, not by sight."*
>
> 2 Corinthians 5:7*

> *"My brethren, count it all joy when you fall into various trials, knowing that the testing of your faith produces patience. But let patience have its perfect work, that you may be perfect and complete, lacking nothing."*
>
> James 1:1-8

---

*Scripture is quoted from the New King James Version, unless otherwise noted.

## Do the Hard Part

What questions do you have for God? Contrary to popular belief, the Bible does not tell us that we cannot question Him. We should not question who He is and His power and capabilities. Questioning God can lead you to the answers that you need to gain peace. Just remember, as you question Him, listen for His voice, because He is sure to respond.

_____

_____

_____

_____

_____

_____

_____

_____

_____

_____

_____

_____

# Chapter Two
## A Time to Grieve

"To every thing there is a season, and a time to every purpose under the heaven: A time to be born, and a time to die; a time to plant, and a time to pluck up that which is planted; A time to kill, and a time to heal; a time to break down, and a time to build up; A time to weep, and a time to laugh; a time to mourn, and a time to dance; A time to cast away stones, and a time to gather stones together; a time to embrace, and a time to refrain from embracing; A time to get, and a time to lose; a time to keep, and a time to cast away; A time to rend, and a time to sew; a time to keep silence, and a time to speak; A time to love, and a time to hate; a time of war, and a time of peace."

---

Ecclesiastes 3:1-8 (KJV)

*I cried uncontrollably for more than a week and I don't recall sleeping or eating much either. The pain was immense and I wouldn't wish it on my worst enemy. I was crying for many reasons from the reality of what had taken place, to my marriage ending so quickly and drastically, and for my girls who also had to go through this transition as well. We all grieved in our own ways whether it were crying or acting out in various spurts of anger, sadness, and a lack of concentration. My youngest took it the hardest because she was the closest to him and didn't quite understand his sudden departure from our home. That was another blow of pain that none of us were prepared for. As a mother we never want to see our children suffer and it hurts even more when there's nothing you can do to take away the pain. I didn't try to control the grief for any of us; I knew that at some point, the grief would end. It couldn't stay forever.*

Experiencing loss whether it's the end of a marriage, relationship, friendship, or the death of a friend or loved one (especially unexpectedly), is a transition period that takes time. Grief is an important step that cannot be skipped or shortened by time simply because we choose not to deal with it. At the same time, grief can't stay longer than God intended. Grief has a season just like everything else in life.

Anyone who has been married and divorced knows that regardless of who was at fault for the dissolution of the marriage, they had to deal with the aftermath of their significant other no longer being in their lives and it still hurt—period. After such a hard blow to my marriage, my heart, and my family, I realized I still had to go through the stages of grief and loss while picking up the pieces.

These stages vary from person-to-person, but typically, grieving involves:

- denial
- anger
- bargaining
- depression
- acceptance

I can tell you I went through all of these stages (multiple times) and rightfully so, but the good part, (yes good part) was that I had the love and word of God to guide me through each stage. I allowed myself (through prayer) time and grace to work through each phase. When the thoughts or actions arose that reverted me back to a particular phase, I dealt with it and continued to deal with it one day at a time. I make no excuse for randomly needing to find a safe private place to cry and pray. That's what God wants from us. He delights and desires for us to run to Him and surrender our thoughts and ways so that He can comfort and strengthen us.

When loss hits (especially unexpectedly) we often want to avoid the feelings and emotions that come along with loss by seeking a means to replace what was lost or simply ignore the subject all together and go on with life as if it didn't happen. I am extremely guilty of this and knew it was time to change my approach. This time, I was determined to learn how to deal with the grief, loss, and the feelings and emotions that came with it; and I owe that to prayer and therapy. It was imperative for me to actually go through the process without feeling like I had to immediately replace that space with another person, tangible items, and even behaviors.

This time around, I utilized prayer as my weapon to help navigate through this loss and therapy was my choice of strategy. Therapy helped me to realize that it's okay to have these feelings and break the cycle of always trying to mask and or avoid those feelings. I learned how to address things head on in a healthy manner.

> *"For God has not given us a spirit of fear, but of power and of love and of a sound mind."*
>
> 2 Timothy 1:7 (ESV)

> *"But I would strengthen you with my mouth, And the comfort of my lips would relieve your grief."*
>
> Job 16:5

In addition to the stages of grief and loss, there is a mourning period. Mourning consists of adapting to life after the loss. For me, it was accepting that I was back to being a single mother. I no longer had my "partner in crime" to talk to about life, work, and politics. I no longer had someone around the house to help with all the things that needed to be done to keep the house functioning. I no longer had my business partner to strategize with. I no longer had my earthly protector and the life I had quickly got accustomed to, and it took some time to readjust. I vividly recall not remembering to put the trash out on pick up days for almost three weeks! During the mourning period, I often reflected on the losses, and my constant reflection led to battles with depression and anxiety. However, the Holy Spirit kept reminding me of the most powerful thing I had, and that was my faith in God. I had faith and hope that He would restore everything at the appointed time. For that to happen, I had to change my mindset first and go back to my pre-marital way of doing things. As painful as it was, it was part of the healing process. Sometimes in life you will have to take several steps backwards, several times, in order to move forward.

*"And God will wipe away every tear from their eyes; there shall be no more death, nor sorrow, nor crying. There shall be no more pain, for the former things have passed away."*
Revelation 21:4

## Do the Hard Part

Reflect in writing on the following questions and prompts. Doing the hard work with confronting your own grief will eventually help you heal and prepare to move forward from this point.

- What were some of the most difficult things about what (or who) you lost and are grieving over?

- How do you cope with it? Do you apply the same process to other matters in your life? If you cannot answer this question, you may want to consider speaking with a loved one, friend, and even possibly seeking professional support services such as therapy or counseling.

_____

_____

_____

_____

_____

_____

_____

_____

# Chapter Three
## Rooted in Faith

"And without faith it is impossible to please him, for whoever would draw near to God must believe that he exists and that he rewards those who seek him."

---

Hebrews 11:6 (ESV)

*From the minute I learned about the abuse, my faith was tested. Naturally, it even wavered for the first few days. I felt like the oil that I placed on the front door of my home and every door inside of my home failed me. But once again I had to remind myself that the oil was a show of faith, not a promise that trouble would never come. The oil was a symbol that even "when you go through deep waters, I will be with you" —Isaiah 48:2.*

*Indeed the first few days and weeks were deep waters, more like a nightmare that just kept going; my life was turned upside down. My prayer had been suddenly answered, and it cost me a lot, but I would soon realize that I was gaining so much more. The actions that needed to take place because of this painful experience was confirmed in the days following when I picked back up on my morning devotional reading.*

A week prior to this event, I had hand selected a new devotional plan that I was to start at the beginning of the week. The devotional that I had selected was sent to a friend in Christ so that we could read together just as we had done a few times before. However, due to the newly developed events, I didn't start reading the plan until three days after the start date. As I was trying to take my mind off things and stay committed, I began reading the devotional plan.

The devotional was dedicated to encouraging women in business, and the first day was titled "You Can't Have a Testimony without a Test." How fitting right? It went on to touch on Joseph's purpose revealed after years of obstacles and Job suffering tremendous loss, and not as punishment, but because he was called and favored by God. The common takeaway for that day's reading was that if God has positioned you to endure a test, regardless of how big, small, painful, and downright embarrassing, trust and believe; He is strengthening your faith, self-control, and patience.

All of these revelations came from the first day of reading the devotional—the devotional that I personally chose one week prior to my life being turned upside down! The devotional I started reading late. From this first day of reading, I was posed with questions such as: What is God currently trying to teach me through this pain? When was the last time I shared a testimony that helped restore hope in someone else? That's when I quickly realized three days into my life being flipped, this was one of many testimonies I had to share. I realized right then, I couldn't continue to encourage others to keep Doin' All Things' without being more transparent. Without my deep rooted faith and relationship with God, I wouldn't have been able to realize this so quickly.

## My Faith Walk

My faith journey began when I was about eight or nine years old while visiting family in Florida. I remember giving my life to Christ but not really knowing what it meant. A few years later, my mother and step father began to attend church more regularly and I started to learn the Bible, but I still didn't have a firm relationship with God or understanding of what it meant to be saved. During my teenage years, I recall the time when I was sent to live with my Pentecostal aunt and her family for approximately six months. My mother was on deployment with the Air Force. Living with a Pentecostal family as a teenager in the mid '90s was a life changing experience, but that was where the foundation of my faith was formed.

As a teenage music lover, I had to immediately switch from loving my boy groups like Immature, Soul For Real, 112, and of course New Edition and my personal favorites such as Mariah Carey, Toni Braxton, and Mary J. Blige. The new music I listened to consisted of Kirk Franklin, Fred Hammond, and Commissioned (who became my favorite gospel music artists). I quickly memorized the books of the Bible in the New Testament as well as a few Bible verses. At a very early age I also learned the importance of praying and fasting. YES, fasting as a youth! We were encouraged even as teenagers to fast one day a week, and I recall Wednesday being my day of choice. As challenging as it was for me as a teenager to accept this new change of life, I'm so grateful for that time with my aunt, uncle, grandmother, and cousins. It was truly the foundation of my walk with God and the reason why now I can quickly find books in the Bible, pray the walls down, and discipline myself to fast. That time spent with my family in Florida is the reason I am able to take the same approach to teaching my nine-year-old how to memorize books of the Bible five at a time, just like I was taught. (My older daughter is ahead of the game and has memorized more than me!)

Having that foundation established at such a young age was necessary. I can honestly say my faith in God was not built on someone just telling me to "believe." My faith walk and relationship with God were built on my own experiences from childhood and high school, through a very adventurous life serving in the Air Force, to starting over in life multiple times as a single mother of two (including one child with special needs). My faith in God was built on my own messy, drama-filled experiences realizing that even through it all, God continued to show up for not only me, but every single member of my family as well.

This current testimony is not flowery at all; it's deep, painful, and it affects not only my life, but my children's as well. Despite how hard this situation is and has been, I remind myself daily that I can "do all things" for the sake of my sanity, for my girls, for my blood line. I can and will be the one to break generational curses. I remind myself that I can show the world how God stepped in to help me and my family heal and eventually forgive, love, and trust again.

> *"Now faith is the assurance of things hoped for, the conviction of things not seen."*
>
> Hebrews 11:1 (ESV)

## Do the Hard Part

Can you trace your faith and track your walk with God? Take a few moments to list some of the major times in your life when God has proved His character of faithfulness. When was the last time you shared one of these experiences with a believer or unbeliever?

# Chapter Four
## Fear Not

"In the multitude of my anxieties within me,
Your comforts delight my soul."

---

Psalm 94:19

*Once reality set in, I slowly began to open up the communication with my girls about the situation. The three of us had some difficult, but much needed, conversations on the reality of things and we made preparations for our new life and what it may look like. That's when fear began to grow in my mind and heart. Fear of starting over, fear of being alone, fear of looking like a failure because of my marriage ending, fear of my girls not being able to love and trust again. This situation was not my fault and I will not take the blame for it, but that didn't stop fear and anxiety from immobilizing me from making many hard decisions, to include what to cook for dinner. We (well the girls) ate out a lot during those first two weeks, but at least they ate, right?*

The devil used fear to continuously remind me that my life would never be the same and that I would never be able to recover or move on from this. (In hindsight, that's the devil's job: to steal, kill, and cause confusion.) During the first few weeks, I was so overwhelmed by the many decisions that had to be made. Due to fear and anxiety, I felt like everything had to be done right away (to include moving into a new home) or I would be making a mistake by not doing anything right away.

Thanks to family and friends, I was reminded that I didn't have to make any decisions right now on that day, or even that week or month for that matter. I decided that my most important priority was keeping a level head (and of course my girls) and I slowed down just enough to simply pray and read more. Prayer and reading changed and saved my life (and my husband's for that matter). Once I filled myself with the word, I became strong, my emotions were stabilized, and I was able to tackle fear and anxiety. I began to read and meditate on Bible verses related to fear and every time the devil tried to attack my mind, I fought back with the word. Don't get me wrong, it was hard at first. I had many sleepless nights (and still do sometimes).

***"Trust in him at all times, you people; pour out your hearts to him, for God is our refuge."***

Psalm 62:8

*"Therefore do not worry about tomorrow, for tomorrow will worry about its own things. Sufficient for the day is its own trouble."*

Matthew 6:34

## Moving Past Fear

Fear will keep you hostage as long as you allow it. Fear has a way of making you feel you are the only one who has gone through your situation and no one will understand you, let alone support you. Coming to the realization that you're not alone regardless of the situation you may find yourself in an essential step in the process of moving forward in healing. Those who really know me know it's typically hard for me to accept support from others. Being the independent woman I am, I often rejected assistance of any kind with a simple "Thank you, but I got it." I was fearful of allowing others near me and my girls just because we had already gone through enough. However, after some point, I realized I would be no good to anyone, including my children, if I was going to continue trying to be a superwoman at a time when I just needed to be a woman.

Let's stop to take a moment to talk about how this event correlates with my brand, Doin' All Things.

*"I can do all things through Christ who strengthens me"*

Philippians 4:13

The Bible tells us that we can do powerful things through His strength; things that may seem impossible on our own merit, but when we call on His name and operate in His power, nothing is impossible. Over the past nine years, I have branded myself without even realizing it to be a woman of encouragement always replying back to family and friends, "Oh you got this. You can do all things!" It wasn't until 2019 when I decided to be more obedient and take it a step further and walk in my gift of encouragement. I successfully developed various social media platforms to include a website dedicated to encouraging others and bringing them to Christ.

It is my belief that there is another component to Doin' All Things. The second component includes empowering others like you and to help take the load off (especially during difficult times) so that you can continue to do all things. I am a firm believer that God will place the right individuals in our lives at the right time to help us carry out His mission. It will take a team, a village, of not just family, but REAL friends to help you through this. Allow others to be there to support you in whatever capacity is needed, whether it be cooking, cleaning, babysitting, or just sitting with you to be a shoulder to cry on or vent to; you never know who needs this opportunity and how being there for you will help them as well.

For example, during the summer before this ordeal began, I started a walking group on Facebook and opened it up to friends and their friends as well. With everything going on during this time, I just wasn't motivated to walk, let alone lead the group and cheer them on. I had already taken an absence from the group for obvious reasons for a few weeks, but as I started to regain my strength, I knew I still wasn't 100 percent ready to get back to the group. I've always noticed one of the members in particular who was consistent with motivating others, and I felt her positive spirit, although I had never actually met her in person. I immediately felt that she was capable of leading the walking group and perhaps taking it to another level. I approached her with my idea to make her co-administrator of the group because of her positive attitude and consistency. Little did I know, she was also going through a life event that involved grief and loss, but accepted the position to keep her mind busy! See how God works? I was approaching her because I needed help, but little did I know, I was actually blessing her with an opportunity at a time when she really needed something positive in her life as well. To this day she is still an active co-administrator for the walking group and has brought so much more life, new members, and motivation to the group. Every time I see one of her posts, I pat myself on the back knowing I made the right choice by releasing some control so that I could continue to focus on putting my life back on track.

Another team or village member that I found to be imperative to my healing journey was a professional therapist. For each person, the help needed may be different, but it still may be helpful to explore seeking professional therapy. I think it is pretty obvious I am a believer of Christ, but I'm also a firm believer in therapy. The Bible teaches us how to live our lives in the spiritual realm, however we are still earthen vessels and it doesn't hurt to seek assistance. I began seeing a therapist in 2018 for issues unrelated to this event and will admit it was about ten years too late. Looking back I wish I had the courage to seek assistance when I REALLY needed it, but I was prideful and confused. I'd heard so many conflicting messages throughout my life, including Christians don't need therapy, we need to pray our problems away. I was confused wondering if I should pursue that avenue for me. When I finally mustered up the courage to begin therapy, it was an eye opener. The groundwork has been set working through feelings and emotions from past events that I never really recovered from and because of that I kept finding myself in the same pattern of behaviors.

When this situation arose, I knew my entire family would need both God and therapy to make it through. I wasted zero time looking for a new therapist that specializes in grief, loss, and trauma for both myself and my family. I needed a therapist who could not only help me through all these things, but one who was also faith based and who understood and respected my choice to have God and therapy.

Aside from praying and writing this book, family therapy was the best decision I made during this time. Returning to regular therapy sessions (after some months off during the beginning of the pandemic) aided in my healing in more ways than one. I was able to acknowledge and process the stages of grief and loss in a healthy manner while making peace with the situation. This included the initial steps to forgiveness and continuing the journey of self reflecting and establishing boundaries in many areas of my life.

Prior to this situation, I made it my mission to have an open door communication policy with my girls so that they can always come to me when something is wrong without fear of reprisal from me. However, I had neglected to teach them that it's also okay to seek a therapist or counselor to talk through things as well. With this new experience we were all going through, I immediately dispelled yet another generational curse, making sure they knew that it's okay if they didn't feel comfortable sharing all of the fine details (of any situation) with me as long as they share with a trusted adult who can help them. Thanks to my obedience to seek therapy during this time, the myth surrounding therapy and the unwillingness to get professional help is another generational curse that will be broken.

Aside from ensuring that therapy was included in the healthing journey for myself and my girls, as preposterous as it may seem, it was equally important to me that I also took the time to help my husband. Yes, my life was turned upside down by this man; however, he was still my husband and I was still called to be the "salt and light" of the world.

> *"But I have prayed for you, that your faith should not fail; and when you have returned to Me, strengthen your brethren."*
>
> Luke 22:32

I chose to support him by helping him locate his own rehabilitation services so that he could finally start the hard work on his issues—issues that arrived way before I entered his life. His issues became mountains during this pandemic and contributed to the abuse that took place.

As I navigate this journey called life, I'm learning more and more that the issues we don't deal with will eventually deal with us. Hurt people, hurt people and that's exactly what happened here. The wound from a painful event may not be your fault, but the healing is definitely your responsibility.

**Author's Note:** If you have reached the point in your life where something is controlling you and you know you are no longer making sound decisions, seek God and seek professional HELP.

*"Be strong and of good courage, do not fear nor be afraid of them; for the Lord your God, He is the One who goes with you. He will not leave you nor forsake you."*

Deuteronomy 31:6

*"Let your light so shine before men, that they may see your good works, and glorify your Father in heaven."*

Matthew 5:16

*"Therefore, whatever you want men to do to you, do also to them, for this is the Law and the Prophets."*

Matthew 7:12

## Do the Hard Part

- How has fear kept you from fulfilling goals and dreams in your life?

- What might be some of the root causes of your fear(s)?

# Chapter Five
## Stop the Thoughts at the Door

"Casting down arguments and every high thing that exalts itself against the knowledge of God, bringing every thought into captivity to the obedience of Christ."

---

2 Corinthians 10:5

*At night, my mind would keep replaying scenarios of the abuse that took place and many other negative memories of my past that I had already moved on from. On the rare occasions that I was able to drift off to sleep (thanks to Melatonin), I would often wake up from nightmares dripped in sweat. On more than one occasion, I stayed up all night as if that would stop the dreams and thoughts. During those all-nighters I prayed my hardest! I refused to let this or anything else take my mind, peace, and joy!*

The devil's main agenda for your life is to keep you in bondage with your thoughts so that your peace is disturbed and joy nonexistent. This is essentially called spiritual warfare. He will throw up past scenarios of past trials and tribulations to show you where you went wrong and how you shouldn't trust God again because "if God loved you so much, He wouldn't allow this to happen right?" I will be honest and say, those were some of the thoughts that ran rampant in my mind.

The devil is familiar with our fears, triggers, and securities and will stop at nothing to keep our minds lingering on those things. This includes taking responsibility for something that may not have been yours to accept in the first place. (If it was yours, it's best to make peace with it as well and seek forgiveness.) Regardless, continuing to reflect on the loss, situation, or storm takes you out of the presence of God and puts you in the hand of the devil himself. That's when and where we start to feel like we can "fix things on our own" just as Sarah did when she became impatient with waiting to become pregnant and brought in a surrogate.

The strongholds that the devil employs to attack your mind can be lifelong battles if you entertain them long enough. As hard as it may be, keep your focus on God. The most effective way to remain focused on the problem solver is through the word and prayer! Yes, you can utilize other methods such as gaining a new hobby, reading, and exercising and while those can be helpful distractions, I can assure you prayer is best. When I sought His face not only for comfort, He gave me direction and it eased my mind tremendously. I also gained a higher level of peace the more I sought God.

> *"For we do not wrestle against flesh and blood, but against principalities, against powers, against the rulers of [a]the darkness of this age, against spiritual hosts of wickedness in the heavenly places."*
>
> Ephesians 6:12

> *"Finally, brethren, whatever things are true, whatever things are noble, whatever things are just, whatever things are pure, whatever things are lovely, whatever things are of good report, if there is any virtue and if there is anything praiseworthy— meditate on these things."*
>
> Philippians 4:8

## Do the Hard Part

Here are some ways to remain in a positive state of mind:

1. Seek God daily; put your mind on the healer and not the problem and/or person.

2. Help others and share your testimony. You never know how much of a blessing you can be to someone else who actually may be experiencing the same situation.

# Chapter Six
## Wait Upon The Lord

"Rejoicing in hope, patient in tribulation, continuing steadfastly in prayer"

Romans 12:12

*Because of fear (which often leads to anxiety), I felt as if I had to pivot quickly so that **I, Andrea,** could heal and move on. One of those immediate changes was to figure out where my girls and I would live. Within the first week, I bought boxes and started packing and didn't even have a new home lined up. I felt as if **I** needed to move on in order to move forward, which wasn't wrong. It just wasn't the right time. I was willing to put all my belongings in storage and move myself and girls in with my mother until I found us a new home. On my daughter's ninth birthday, hours before her party was to start and exactly one week after all hell broke loose, I was out looking at homes with my mother. It was one of the biggest mistakes of my life. I'm sure she saw through the fact that my mind may have been ready to start looking, but my heart wasn't. I had to refocus very quickly on what we needed as a family of three, versus four. We no longer needed a massive single family home, which included my own office space, basement, and a three-car garage. Now, a much smaller home was more fitting for our family. It was a hard adjustment and I struggled tremendously with the reality.*

There were quite a few things wrong with the thought process of "I, Andrea" and what I, Andrea needed. The first part and probably the worst part of thinking like this was of course the "I" part. I was leaving Him, God, out of everything. I had not yet prayed about the decisions I was making. The second problem with the thought process of "I, Andrea" was that I was rushing things for Andrea and not even considering my girls and how they felt. I'm sure a lot of parents from older generations will not agree with what I'm about to say next, but it was important to me to have some feedback from my girls about how they felt about this situation and our next move, so I spoke with them individually about each subject so that they could have my undivided attention and responses. My girls are different ages and have completely different comprehension levels, so it was important (and still is) to meet them at their levels. After a series of conversations, I learned that they both were actually okay with staying in our current home for the time being and that took 1,000 bricks of stress off of my shoulders. I was on the cusp of disrupting their lives and their routines (even more so than what had already been done) for my own selfish reasons.

Making life changing decisions during a storm requires a sound mind. I do not recommend anyone making decisions while their emotions are unstable (especially if it affects others who are close to you). Instead, I suggest that you pray and wait upon the Lord and wait as long as it takes! I learned this lesson during my downtime of "being still." During those late nights and early morning prayer sessions, I wholeheartedly sought Him asking for His will and not my own and through the voices of my girls, He spoke to me and said "wait, I will restore."

As I continued to seek Him, my mind became clearer. I was no longer constantly overcome by fear; my mind was slowly being replaced with *power, love, and a sound mind*. Fear and anxiety were slowly leaving. Day by day, He began to restore my peace, direction, and counsel and He even included sprinkles of joy and hope. I remember very vividly early one morning before my girls woke up. I was drinking coffee, praying, and reading. He spoke to me and said, "If I answered your prayers regarding this situation, then what makes you think I won't answer your prayers for healing?" When we wait, God provides us with clarity and answers!

As the days, weeks, and life itself rolled by with distance learning for the girls and work for me, I also regained my strength and confidence with making decisions and the same will happen for you. When the timing is right, you will have to make some major decisions even when the outcome is uncertain. That's when you have to activate your faith, especially when you're in the middle of the storm because there's no expiration date for the turmoil. In the wilderness of the quiet moments when you think He's not listening or working things out, He is. The storm will end when He's ready, therefore I encourage you to continue praying for His will to be done and release the results to Him.

All too often we get ahead of God planning a way out. That's when we make mistakes. He gives us enough grace and strength for each day, but it's up to us to operate in it.

Had I rushed into moving myself and girls to my mother's, who knows what could've happened. That wasn't what God had planned for us. I could've missed out on a major part of the healing process by trying to skip ahead, and I could've missed out on more blessings by simply moving too soon. I recently heard a message from T.D. Jakes titled "God Knows When." In that message I was reminded that God is all knowing and He knows the right time to move forward. He has a plan for everything and it will be revealed at the right time. Wait upon the Lord!

*"But those who wait on the Lord Shall renew their strength; They shall mount up with wings like eagles, They shall run and not be weary, They shall walk and not faint."*

Isaiah 40:31

*"We can make our plans, but the Lord determines our steps."*

Proverbs 16:9 (NLT)

*"And you will seek Me and find Me, when you search for Me with all your heart."*

Jeremiah 29:13

## Do the Hard Part

Are you anxious to move ahead of God? Take a moment to pause and consider the potential consequences of moving too soon and potential blessings of waiting on God's timing.

# Chapter Seven
## Letting Go of Anger and Forgiving Others

"I have decided to stick to love…Hate is too great a burden to bear."

---

Dr. Martin Luther King Jr.

*Despite what had been done, I still spoke with my husband by phone daily during the first few weeks. Some family and even friends did not agree with this, but that was my decision. I felt as if I needed answers from him and he was going to hear every emotion I was dealing with; good, bad, ugly and regardless of the time of the day. And he did; he listened and apologized every day, regardless of the time of day. We cried a lot on the phone together during the first few weeks. I was hurt, heartbroken, angry, and rightfully so. The more I prayed, the more I realized that at some point I had to give the hurt and pain to God.*

I stated before that hurtful actions come from hurting people and it was important to me to exercise grace and humanity and get to the root of the problem(s). It will take a tremendous amount of prayer and a mature walk with God to put aside your own feelings, allow the love of God to flow through you, still love the person who wronged you, and accept the storm for what it is. Yep, I said it. As a believer, it is your responsibility to love the person who hurt you with or without a closure or an apology from them. (Notice, I didn't say return to the person that wronged you).

It will take time to accept what has happened regardless of the situation and find ways to see God in it. This is still part of His divine plan as painful as it maybe. I know first hand, loving and accepting are much easier said than done, but we are talking about Doin' All Things...right? That means Doin' All Things in His name, through His strength, and for His glory, not our own. I've heard multiple times from my pastor, Pastor John K. Jenkins Jr. of First Baptist Church of Glenarden, to hate the sin not the sinner, and I believe it to be true. Moving past anger after this situation especially when the anger is truly justified is just like forgiveness; it's more for you than the person who hurt you. It's imperative during this season to not allow the anger, hatred, and bitterness to consume you. If that happens, you will have another mountain to wrestle with and that is not what you need right now.

*"Darkness cannot drive out darkness; only light can do that. Hate cannot drive out hate; only love can do that."*

Dr. Martin Luther King Jr.

*"My command is this: Love each other as I have loved you."*

John 15:12 (NIV)

*"Above all, love each other deeply, because love covers over a multitude of sins."*

1 Peter 4:8 (NIV)

## Do the Hard Part

- Be honest with yourself. Have you allowed anger to take precedent over your love, kindness, gentleness, patience (long-suffering), and self-control that the Lord has called you to display as a child of God?

- Today, how can you put aside your anger (and even perhaps hatred) to put your relationship with God and personal healing first?

# Chapter Eight
## Forgiveness

"For if you forgive other people when they sin against you, your heavenly Father will also forgive you."

---

Matthew 6:14 (NIV)

*I know I am fully capable of forgiving someone, because there are quite a few times in my life when I've chosen to walk in forgiveness. However, this situation is completely different from anything I've ever been through and, initially, forgiveness was the furthest thing from my mind. I actually refused to forgive him and accept his apologies initially. My own behavior and inability to forgive contradicted what I've been taught and am teaching to my girls. This kept me up many nights...that along with wanting to take vengeance into my own hands.*

I want to be completely honest with you right now. At this point in my life as I'm writing this book one month in, I haven't forgiven my husband for turning my life upside down. Yes, I still helped him begin his own healing journey, but that doesn't mean I have forgiven. Through working with my therapist, I have realized and accepted this is not my fault. She continues to encourage me to start the forgiveness process by first forgiving myself for the things I didn't know, so I want to tell you the same thing. Forgive yourself for not knowing what you know now.

After forgiving yourself, you will start to feel more peace about the storm even while still in the storm! I also received wisdom from attending regular therapy sessions. This is where I learned to consistently reflect on how far I've come regarding this event and past events. The fact that I have forgiven people in the past validates that it can be done again regardless of the situation. For me forgiveness is a spiritual component and not for the faint at all. It's a daily practice and gets easier as the days go by. When we choose to walk in forgiveness, it's not for the other person's sake; it's for our own.

Here's what I've learned and have had to exercise about forgiveness:

1. You can forgive but not forget.
2. You can forgive and not return back to that friendship and/or relationship.
3. When you choose to forgive, it's not healthy to continue to remind the individual (or yourself) about the incident.

***"And whenever you stand praying, if you have anything against anyone, forgive him, that your Father in heaven may also forgive you your trespasses."***

Mark 11:25

## Do the Hard Part

Forgiveness is not easy. In fact, Jesus, as He hung on the cross preparing to take His last breath, forgave those who had persecuted and killed him. During the final moments of the most difficult act that has ever been done on behalf of mankind, forgiveness was present. Though it was most difficult, this was also the greatest display of love ever realized. Christ is our example, through love, for forgiveness, in suffering. Are you able to forgive the person or people who hurt you so that you too can experience a resurrection in your life?

# Chapter Nine
## Prayer Changed Me

"Therefore I tell you, whatever you ask in prayer, believe that you have received it, and it will be yours."

---

Mark 11:24 (NIV)

*In all transparency, I had begun to notice some behavioral changes within my husband's overall mood and demeanor during the summer. I confronted him multiple times regarding this and the responses were always the same. So I took it to prayer like I always did. During my morning walks, I prayed fervently for him and the state of our marriage. I sensed things were turning and I was no longer confident about our marriage lasting beyond the pandemic. There were many other contributing factors to me feeling this way; private conversations between me and God. I continued to pray about everything and there were quite a few times I saw the evidence of my prayers being answered through my husband's actions and my own response in how I handled things. Then there were times when it was only God Himself who knew my secret thoughts and turned them into blessings. That's how amazing He is. He even knows our thoughts and responds to them accordingly!*

Prayer has been my saving grace the past few months. I've prayed more than I have my entire life. I owe that all to my time spent living with my Pentecostal aunt. In addition to learning how to fast, I also learned how to seek God with my whole heart through prayer. Friday night prayer attendance was a must while I was living with her. The lights were dim and light worship music flowed creating an atmosphere for God to show up and He did each and every night. For those that could kneel, we did. We would kneel at the altar or in our respective areas of the church and we prayed the walls down. Therefore, God had prepared me for such a time as this! I'm a prayer warrior and pray over any and everything these days. I continue to rise early each day to find my quiet place and talk with Him, and our time often involves worship music and coffee. I don't just stop there; I pray all throughout the day; prayer has been essential to my healing journey.

Needless to say, when I say prayer changed me, I'm not just referring to just this event, but in other instances too. I can recall countless times when I had been praying for a certain individual to change their ways. I would pray, "I wish this person would be more of this or that," but in the midst of me praying, God used those prayers to change me! That person didn't necessarily change and neither did the situation. However, my approach and how I chose to deal with the situation changed. Instead of saying, 'I wish this person were more of this or that,' I became more of what I wished they were. Through prayer, I learned to extend more grace to individuals and myself as well.

Another component with prayer is patience. There's a lot to be said during the waiting season when you pray. It will literally either break you in your walk with God or build you up and make you stronger. During my waiting season there were so many times I actually questioned if God was even listening to me. The thing about prayer, however, is that God answers when He's ready—or better yet, when He knows we're ready to receive everything He has for us. His answers to our prayers may not exactly look like what we perceived, therefore we must prepare for what we pray for regardless of the response.

Ironically, right after hell broke loose, my mother gave me a book titled *When Women Pray* by T.D. Jakes and it was life changing! I spoke about it intensively on my social media page and even gifted a few women copies of it because it blessed me so much. There are so many lessons and nuggets in this book, however the one that spoke to me the most was a section titled Secret Whispers. It says that God's ability to act is not dependent on our ability to pray.

> *"Sometimes God hears the secret whispers of our heart, even when those secrets don't escape our lips. He knows all things up to the thoughts in our minds and the longings in our hearts. There are times that God chooses to react to those longings, even with no request from us." (page 45)*

Other lessons about prayer that I learned from this book and my own personal experiences are:

1. Having a designated place to pray is important. For me it's in the corner of my living room mostly in the early mornings with a prayer mat, or just walking around my home.

2. Through prayer I learned how to be quiet and listen to Him provide His counsel, direction, and comfort for my life. Prayer is not always about us unloading our problems on Him and expecting miracles; there's power in being still.

3. Prayer helps us regain our strength.

4. Creating and using a prayer box can be helpful. A prayer box (or jar) is a safe place to keep track of your prayers. Simply write them on a piece of paper, deposit them into the box (or jar); and walk away and allow God to do His work. Revisit the jar either once or twice a year and reflect on the goodness of God!

Prayer is the ultimate line of communication between you and God. He doesn't need our prayers to be complicated or sound like a doctoral project either. There have been many instances in my life when I have said things during prayer that were not politically correct, Christian-like and even lady-like for that matter. Our prayers don't have to be perfect, just sincere. Our prayers don't have to be long, just sincere. Our prayers don't have to be done at the same time everyday, just sincere. Our prayers don't have to be done in public, just sincere. Our prayers only need to be sincere.

> ***"Be anxious for nothing, but in everything by prayer and supplication, with thanksgiving, let your requests be made known to God."***
>
> Philippians 4:6

> ***"Now this is the confidence that we have in Him, that if we ask anything according to His will, He hears us."***
>
> 1 John 5:14

## Do the Hard Part

Most often, we complain, worry, or get angry before we pray, when prayer changes situations more often than these other activities. Take a moment to think about your conversations and thoughts this week. What have you neglected to pray about? What situations have you complained or worried about without spending the adequate time in prayer? Write a prayer list for yourself, especially for these situations.

# Chapter Ten
## Self-Care

Self-care: the practice of taking an active role in protecting one's own well-being and happiness, in particular during periods of stress.

*Almost two months to the day of me learning about everything, I posted on social media that "I needed a momcation, even if it's just for twenty-four hours." I received a ton of "likes" and comments from my mom-friends expressing the same sentiments. In their minds, we could relate to each other because this new life of working from home and homeschooling was wearing us out! Some of that is true, but adding the level of stress I was personally dealing with during the previous two months is something I wouldn't wish on my worst enemy. My post was really a silent cry of sorts, and I really was screaming out for help, because I was on my way to having a nervous breakdown!*

*It had been the longest two months of my life, and I was "handling things so well." According to loved ones, I was "so strong," and they were "so proud" of me. The truth is it really just sucks being a strong woman of God. It's painful having to get up each day to face the world. It's painful to be forced to make so many difficult adult decisions when all I really wanted to do is stay in bed to sleep, rest, and not have to think about everything.*

*Over the previous two months, I hadn't gotten much rest and it was finally starting to affect my health. My calm and sweet demeanor was starting to unfold along with my patience. However, I kept going, going, and going and even pushed myself to attend a holiday event as a vendor for my business Doin' All Things (which turned out to be very successful), but afterwards, I waved my white flag in the need of twenty-four hours, kid-free!*

As a mother, I found it was imperative to keep my children's routine as normal as possible. I have two girls and my youngest has autism. Distance learning was still in session for my third and eighth graders due to the ongoing pandemic. As determined as I was to keep life going, I realized I needed to also allow myself some grace at the same time. I decided that no matter what, I wouldn't let myself go completely. I needed to keep my self-care up now more than ever, but I also knew I didn't need to stress over it at the same time, if that makes sense.

Prior to this, I had a "Self-care Sundays" ritual that I took very seriously. Sunday evenings after my family ate dinner and the kitchen was clean, I would retreat to the tub and have the best and bubbliest bath to include a glass of wine! With the turn of events, I continued this ritual except it happened everyday (minus the wine) like clockwork. Being immersed in water has always given me a sense of peace, and sitting in a tub filled with relaxing aromatherapy scents and bubbles was no different.

During the first few weeks, I didn't have much of an appetite and unconsciously lost all of my quarantine weight and then some. Those first few weeks were the saddest weeks of my life and I cried everyday, all day. Then I began to cry, pray, read, and write, which ended up being the best form of self-care that I could imagine. I allowed myself to feel every emotion and deal with them in a positive manner.

It took an incredible amount of time to get back to the other parts of me that I enjoyed prior to this event. I mentioned before that I didn't have the energy to cook for almost two weeks. I now had the time, but still lacked the desire and learned to be okay with how I felt. Even keeping up with personal hygiene seems like a no brainer, but you would be surprised at what you let slip while you're going through hard times Nevertheless as the weeks went by, I slowly started to feel like myself and even began to "get dressed" daily. Keep in mind again, during a pandemic "getting dressed" consisted of my everyday attire of a Doin' All Things shirt and leggings, earrings, and mascara. But with each step forward, there were five steps back. As much as I put on the front that I was "getting better," the lack of real sleep and rest was still absent and starting to weigh me down. I had even created a horrible habit of needing several over the counter medications just to guide me to sleep, and none of them really worked. In hindsight, they didn't work because God was showing me how to lean and depend on Him and Him alone.

Keeping up with the "Andrea, you're doing so well" perception was tiring. I was exhausted! Emotionally exhausted. I was burned out due to the restless nights, long work days and stress over finances, all while trying to maintain the facade that everything was alright. Burnout causes people to feel drained, unable to cope, and tired. They often lack the energy to get their work done. As the prayer warrior that I am, I included the need for sleep in my prayers and not just any type of sleep, but peaceful sleep!

> ***"Come to Me, all you who labor and are heavy laden, and I will give you rest."***
>
> Matthew 11:28

If you have noticed, the term "self-care" has become more commonly used in the last few years, however, I would say that self-care varies from person-to-person. I have compiled a list of my favorite self-care ideas that change my mood instantly.

1. Drink an herbal tea
2. Try a face mask
3. Take a walk
4. Watch my favorite show
5. Take myself out for a date night
6. Read inspirational quotes
7. Watch the sunrise or sunset
8. Do something nice for someone
9. Take a bubble bath
10. Listen to my favorite song at least five times in a row

# Chapter Eleven
## It is Well with My Soul

"I praise you because I am fearfully and wonderfully made; your works are wonderful, I know that full well."

---

Psalm 139:14 (NIV)

*One of my biggest prayers during those dark moments was for healing, peace, and joy to be restored to me and my girls. I can truly say we're all about eighty percent there and I give God all the credit for this. Our lives will never be the same because of this season that we experienced.*

*"My brethren, count it all joy when you fall into various trials, knowing that the testing of your faith produces patience. But let patience have its perfect work, that you may be perfect and complete, lacking nothing."*
*James 1:2-4*

# Perfect Peace

Perfect peace for me consists of having my prayers answered regarding a certain situation. Having this type of peace cost a lot, but I also gained a lot. I have peace of mind now knowing that I made the best decision. I chose the safety and well being of my children and my peace above everything else and that's all that matters.

Had this happened four or five years ago, I know that I would not have been mature enough in my faith to handle this. In all transparency, I know I would have reacted differently, possibly even detrimentally, to more than one person. Had this happened years ago, I wouldn't have been as mentally and spiritually strong as to not only keep going, but to also share this story. I would have been too concerned with the thoughts and opinions of others. People will assume what they want and that's okay. The only person I'm concerned with is God and doing what God has instructed me to do.

The ability to continue to focus on the problem solver (God) has been an intricate part of my peace, and you will find this to be the case for you as well. I have peace now knowing that my girls and I are no longer in harm's way. Going through this with my daughters shows them they are not exempt from life's trials even at their young ages. I also have peace knowing my girls are as resilient as I am. Peace is not a solidarity moment of being happy or having life in order exactly how you would like it. Perfect peace for me comes from knowing that even in the midst of the storm, I'm protected and will be okay.

*"You will keep him in perfect peace, whose mind is stayed on You, because he trusts in you."*

Isaiah 26:3 (ESV)

*"Now may the God of hope fill you with all joy and peace believing that you may abound in hope by the power of the Holy Spirit."*

Romans 15:13 (NIV)

## Do the Hard Part

- What does peace look like to you?
- Are you equating peace to happiness?

# Chapter Twelve
## Moving Forward

I wrote seventy-five percent of this book within the first few weeks into my storm. As I mentioned before, there were many sleepless nights leading me into deep prayer and time to write. Sharing my story has aided in my healing process as well as forgiveness towards him. Over time, healing has taken place and I've learned to give myself more credit and realize how incredibly resilient I am. And because of all this, my girls are also on their own healing journey and just as resilient. Our home is still filled with love, joy, and most importantly, peace. Generational curses have been broken in our family. In our home, we no longer mask and avoid pain here. We present it to God through prayer, let Him handle it, and continue to keep *Doin' All Things, When Life Hurts.*

### Last Words

I sincerely pray this book has given you the strength to keep moving through your storm. Address the pain, grief, and loss. Address the anger, hatred, and even guilt if you carry it. Address it all, then give it to God. In addition to what has already been provided, I also want to offer you my prayers of comfort during this difficult time. If you are like me and have been affected by a domestic abuse situation, know that you're not alone and please seek assistance.

# Scripture Index

**Trust**
Jeremiah 29:11
Proverbs 16:9:7
John 5:14

**Faith**
Romans 10:17
2 Corinthians 5:7
James 1:1-8
Hebrews 11:1,6

**Grief & Loss**
Ecclesiastes 3:1-8
2 Timothy 1:7
Job 16:5
Revelation 21:4

**Fear & Anxiety**
Psalm 94:19, 62:8
Matthew 6:34
2 Corinthians 10:5
Philippians 4:6,8
Deuteronomy 31:6

**Prayer**
Mark 11:24
Psalm 139:14
Ephesians 6:12

**Forgiveness**
Matthew 6:14
Mark 11:25

**Helps**
Luke 22:32
Matthew 5:16

**Love**
John 15:12
1 Peter 4:8
Matthew 7:12

**Patience**
James 1:2-4
Romans 12:12
Jeremiah 29:13
Isaiah 40:31

**Peace**
Isaiah 26:3
Romans 15:13

# Resources

Domestic abuse, also called "domestic violence," can be defined as a pattern of behavior in any relationship that is used to gain or maintain power and control over an intimate partner. Abuse includes physical, sexual, emotional, economic, or psychological actions or threats of actions that influence another person. This includes any behaviors that frighten, intimidate, terrorize, manipulate, hurt, humiliate, blame, injure, or wound someone. Domestic abuse can happen to anyone of any race, age, sexual orientation, religion, or gender. It can occur within a range of relationships including couples who are married, living together, or dating. Domestic abuse affects people of all socioeconomic backgrounds and education levels.

If you have been affected by domestic abuse in any type of way, or know someone that has, please know you are not alone and that there are resources available for you to connect with.

**https://www.thehotline.org**

**1.800.799.SAFE (7233)TTY 1.800.787.3224.**

If you are struggling with substance abuse and mental health issues, or know someone that is, please know that there are resources available for you to connect with. Substance Abuse and Mental Health Services Administration's National Helpline is a free, confidential, 24/7, 365-day-a-year treatment referral and information service (in English and Spanish) for individuals and families facing mental and/or substance use disorders.

**https://www.samhsa.gov/find-help/national-helpline**

**1-800-662-HELP (4357).**

# Stay Connected

## Find Us Online:

Website: www.doinallthings.com
Email: doinallthings@gmail.com
Facebook: /doinallthings
Instagram: @doinallthings
Twitter: @doinallthings

## Want to Leave a Review?

If you've been blessed by this book, please leave a review on our website and perhaps a brief testimony of your own.

## Speaking Requests

Author Andrea Mitchell has over fifteen years of public speaking experience and is available to speak at events serving as keynote speaker, moderator, panelist host, and event host in both private and corporate/government settings.

Speaking topics include, but are not limited to:

- Being a Woman of Faith
- Motherhood (to include single parenting and co-parenting)
- Marriage and Divorce
- Autism Acceptance
- Surviving Domestic Violence

For inquiries, contact Ms. Mitchell at: doinallthings@gmail.com for a free consultation.

www.ingramcontent.com/pod-product-compliance
Lightning Source LLC
Chambersburg PA
CBHW071624170426
43195CB00038B/2116